Lake Ontario

Great Lakes of North America

Harry Beckett

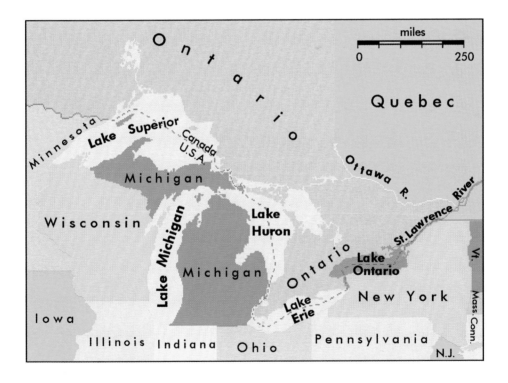

The Rourke Corporation, Inc.
Vero Beach, Florida 32964

PHOTO CREDITS:
Photographs by kind permission of: Geovisuals (Waterloo, Ontario);
Huronia Museum, Midland, Ontario; National Archives of Canada; Fort
Niagara State Park; Thousand Island Bridge Authority; Thousand Islands
International Tourism Council; Rochester; Rapid Magazine, Scott
MacGregor; Michigan Sea Grant; Toronto Police Museum; City of Hamilton
Archives; Maps by J. David Knox

CREATIVE SERVICES:
East Coast Studios, Merritt Island, Florida

EDITORIAL SERVICES:
Susan Albury

Library of Congress Cataloging-in-Publication Data

Beckett, Harry, 1936-
     Lake Ontario / by Harry Beckett.
        p. cm. — (Great Lakes of North America)
     Includes bibliographical references and index.
     Summary: Discusses Lake Ontario's geography, history, early
inhabitants, important events, economy, and more.
        ISBN 0-86593-526-2
     1. Ontario, Lake Juvenile literature. [1. Ontario, Lake.] I. Title. II. Series:
Beckett, Harry, 1936- Great Lakes of North America.
F556.B43 1999
977—dc21
                                                                99-13175
                                                                CIP

Printed in the USA

TABLE OF CONTENTS

About Lake Ontario 5

Native Peoples and Early Explorers 9

Towns and Cities 13

Working Around the Lake 17

Disasters and Mysteries 21

Interesting Places 25

Glossary 31

Index 32

Further Reading 32

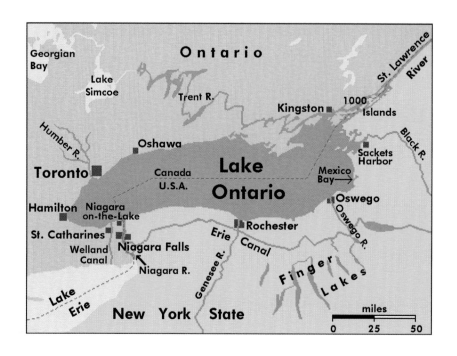

FACTS AND FIGURES FOR LAKE ONTARIO

Length	193 miles	311 kilometers
Width	53 miles	85 kilometers
Average depth	283 feet	86 meters
Maximum depth	802 feet	244 meters
Volume	393 cubic miles	1,640 cubic kilometers
Water surface area	7,340 sq. miles	18,960 sq. kilometers
Shoreline (inc. islands)	712 miles	1,146 kilometers
Area of basin	24,720 sq. miles	64,030 sq. kilometers
Height above sea level	243 feet	74 meters
Retention time*	6 years	

* The average time that it takes for a molecule of water to enter and leave the lake.

ABOUT LAKE ONTARIO

Lake Ontario is the smallest but the second deepest Great Lake. The state of New York is to its south and the province of Ontario to its north. At its western end, it is only 66 miles (105 kilometers) from Georgian Bay and the upper lakes. It receives its water from Lake Erie via the Niagara River and is also linked to Erie by the Welland Canal. Other feeder rivers are the Genesee, Oswego, and Black in New York State, and the Trent and Humber in Ontario. It is the farthest east, and has the lowest altitude of the Great Lakes, 243 feet (74 meters) above sea level.

Because it is the last in the chain of lakes stretching back to Lake Superior, it has the disadvantage of receiving pollution from all the others.

The lake lies in a rocky basin, and the shore is mostly rock or low cliffs with a narrow beach. In Toronto's eastern suburbs, the Scarborough Bluffs rise to 325 feet (100 meters). There are wide sandy beaches between Toronto and Hamilton, and at Mexico Bay in New York State.

The eastern end of the lake has beaches, streams, ponds, bays, and wetlands sheltered behind a coastal barrier of very low limestone rock covered with wet grassland and trees. Wetlands are areas with water standing at or near the land surface for at least part of the year. There are four types of wetland: swamps, marshes, bogs, and fens. They provide **habitats** (HAB uh tats) for many kinds of plants, fish, and animals. They also control pollution and prevent erosion and flooding.

A huge laker carrying cargo along the Waterway

Water flows out of the lake into the Saint Lawrence River in the northeastern corner. At this point, ships are 1,200 miles (1,920 kilometers) from the sea and 1,142 miles (1,827 kilometers) from the western end of Superior. Ontario is thought to be an Iroquoian word meaning "beautiful lake" or "shining water."

The coastal barrier at the east end of the lake.

Native Peoples And Early Explorers

At the time of first contact with European explorers, five nations, the Cayuga, Mohawk, Oneida, Onondaga, and Seneca lived to the south of Lake Ontario. They had lived as warring neighbors until Hiawatha, an Onandaga, met a prophet named Deganawidah, or the Peacemaker. Both men had a vision of the five tribes living in peace. They persuaded them to stop feuding, to form the Iroquois **Confederacy** (kun FED uh ruh see), and to fight against common enemies.

Their united force of ten thousand was able to defeat their northern neighbors, the Neutral, the Petun, and even the more numerous and powerful Huron. They fought because fighting was a way of proving one's courage, but also because they wanted to challenge the Huron for the trade routes. The Neutral lived around Niagara until driven out by the Seneca who were called the "keepers of the western gate."

The Iroquois built their villages near water where the soil was fertile and canoe routes allowed them to trade or make war easily. They built longhouses using bent trees as frames and bark as a covering. Several families lived together in a longhouse. They lived by farming, growing mostly corn, squash, and beans, which they called the three sisters. They only moved when the soil became unfertile. The role of women was very important in Iroquois society.

Étienne Brulé was the first European known to have visited Lake Ontario, in 1615. Samuel de Champlain also traveled the area. He made friends with the Huron, gave them guns, and supported them against the Iroquois.

A Huron brave of the early sixteen hundreds

The Dutch who were rivals of the French and the British in the fur trade, gave guns to the Iroquois, and the way nations fought each other changed.

Because of the conflicts over the fur trade, Europeans only settled the Lake Ontario basin after the British took control in 1763. Many of the first settlers were **Loyalists** (LOY uhl ists), those who were still loyal to the King of England, coming from the United States after the revolution.

An Iroquois council fire

TOWNS AND CITIES

Nearly a quarter of all Canadians live near Lake Ontario, mostly in Toronto (population 4,628,883), the capital of Ontario. Ottawa, the capital of Canada, is also in Ontario. Toronto was once very British but recent immigrants have given it interesting ethnic neighborhoods and a new and lively face. Toronto is a city of activities. Science and technology are a hands-on experience at the Ontario Science Centre, and you can make dinosaurs from chicken bones or visit an Iroquoian longhouse at the Royal Ontario Museum.

From the lively Harbourfront, ferries carry visitors to Centre Island with its many attractions. Exhibition Place, built on stilts and islands in the lake, has children's playgrounds, water parks, concerts, and an Imax theater. Standing on the glass floor of the Space Deck of the C.N. Tower and looking down at the ground, 1,465 feet (447 meters) below, is scary. Those interested in history can tour rebuilt Old Fort York, which once commanded the approach to the U.S. border

A stretch of heavily populated shoreline, called the "Golden Horseshoe," forms an arc around the western end of the lake from Oshawa to St. Catharines. It is the gateway to the Niagara Peninsula. Hamilton (population 451,665) stands at the bottom of the horseshoe. The old town was built on the narrow plain, sandwiched between the **Niagara escarpment** (ni AG ruh eh SKARP munt) and the lake. The city has now spread onto the "mountain." Saint Catharines has an important position on the Welland Canal that connects Lake Ontario to Lake Erie and the West.

The Sesame Street Exhibit at the Strong Museum in Rochester, New York

Rochester (population 231,636) is a deepwater port on the New York shore at the mouth of the Genesee River and on the Erie Canal. It is a cultural, educational, and research center. The Strong Museum and the Rochester Museum and Science Center are popular with children. The home of George Eastman, the pioneer of photography, is now the International Museum of Photography. The Dryden Theater there shows classic movies. The home of Susan B. Anthony, the suffragist, is another museum. Frederick Douglass, escaped slave, orator, and abolitionist, lived for a time in Rochester.

Toronto, with the Island Airport, C.N. Tower, and Skydome

WORKING AROUND THE LAKE

Most of the industry on the lake is concentrated around the Golden Horseshoe. Hamilton has two of Canada's largest steel producers. Much of their steel goes to major automobile and auto parts manufacturers in Oshawa, Oakville, Toronto, and Saint Catharines or to the many manufacturing industries of the region. It is also exported to the United States and beyond. Hamilton is the home of international companies that produce farm machinery, household appliances, glass, and automobile tires.

Toronto is important for its manufacturing but it is becoming more important for its financial power, office-service sector, and hi-tech industries. Several national banks, insurance companies, and national newspaper chains have their headquarters there.

Rochester, in New York State, is a world leader in the production of photographic equipment. The manufacture of optical parts and copying and scientific equipment have earned it the title of the "world's image center." Milling flour from grain from the Genesee Valley was once a major activity. The industry has since moved and been replaced by mail-order seeds and shrub sales. Fruit grown around the city is also processed in Rochester. Its strategic position on two water routes once made it a "boom town of the West."

Trucks and rail cars now carry a lot of the cargoes once moved by ships from the ports, but water transportation is still important, especially for bulk cargoes.

Many of the cities are transshipment ports. They receive deliveries such as grain, ore, petroleum, wood pulp and lumber.

Sacket's Harbor is an important historical and tourism center.

They export things that they produce, such as aluminum or paper from Oswego, dental and electrical equipment from Rochester, or fruit from St. Catharines.

Fishing was once an important industry but it has been badly affected by pollution and **lampreys** (LAM prees). Stocking the lakes is helping them to recover. Like all the lakes, Ontario has a busy tourist industry, both on the water and in its cities.

An iron and steel plant in Hamilton. Iron and coal are brought here by ship.

DISASTERS AND MYSTERIES

The 385-foot (128-meter) cruise ship *Noronic*, with 524 passengers and a crew of 171, arrived in Toronto Harbor at 6 PM on Friday, September 16, 1949. She was due to leave the next evening to cruise the Thousand Islands. Most of the passengers and crew who went ashore had returned to their cabins by midnight. At 1:15 AM, a passenger alerted a steward about smoke coming from a linen closet. When the men opened the door, flames rushed out.

Unable to put out the fire, they raised the alarm. The captain tried using water hoses without success. The ship burned like tinder. The Toronto Fire Department battled the flames for five hours. Many of the passengers became lost as they tried to escape. The crew was able to help save four hundred and eight people before they themselves escaped. But no one could help the one hundred and sixteen who died.

On August 7, 1813, a U.S. fleet sailed out of Niagara-on-the-Lake to challenge a British fleet. By evening, the wind had dropped and the two sides were **becalmed** (buh KAHLMD). They could see each other but were too far apart to fight. During the early morning, a sudden storm capsized the American schooners *Scourge* (10 guns) and *General Hamilton* (10 guns), with great loss of life. They were not built to carry guns and the weight on their decks perhaps unbalanced them. In 1975, divers discovered the wrecks almost intact and they have been featured on television programs. There are sailors who believe that they sail on as ghost ships.

A passenger is lowered from the deck of the burning Noronic.

In November 1780, the Royal Navy sloop *Ontario* left Oswego with between 172 and 350 soldiers and sailors and, some say, $500,000 in gold and silver on board. She was never seen again. The only trace ever found was a drum or, in other reports, a soldier's cap.

The General Hamilton *leaves harbor*

INTERESTING PLACES

The Thousand Islands crowd the Saint Lawrence River on the U.S.-Canada border downstream from Kingston, Ontario. There are up to 1,800 rocky and often tree-covered islands, ranging in size from Wolfe Island, 49 square miles (127 square kilometers), to tiny islets. There are excursion boats and helicopter tours, and homes, cottages, and campgrounds where Iroquois once liked to hunt and fish and where naval battles were fought.

Boldt Castle, on Heart Island, is a 120-room castle complete with tunnels and drawbridge. The Thousand Islands International Bridge links New York State's highways to those of Ontario and Quebec and makes travel to this beautiful area easy.

Every day in season, "British Redcoats" reenact **skirmishes** (SKUR mish shiz), musket drills, and cannon firings at Fort Henry in Kingston.

At Sackets Harbor, the United States fought two battles against the British in the War of 1812, and thousands of troops and sailors once manned the garrison. The Village Center, Battlefield, and Madison Barracks have been restored to become part of the New York State Heritage Area System. Now this former military settlement is an interesting tourist town.

Boldt Castle on Heart Island

Though Oswego's role as a lake port at the northern end of the New York State Barge Canal system is less important than it was, its waters give visitors a chance to kayak and canoe, brave white-water rapids, or dive down to see old wrecks. Fort Ontario has been rebuilt as a New York Historical Site, and costumed **interpreters** (in TUR pruh turz) help visitors recall the years of 1868 to 1869. From 1944 to 1946, it was used to house World War II refugees.

The Niagara River flows into Lake Ontario from a wide gorge. The oldest building on the lakes, the restored French Castle of Fort Niagara, stands high on the U.S. shore. Students can "join" George III's army and learn drills and tactics from uniformed instructors. Across the river in Niagara-on-the-Lake, Fort George is within cannon shot.

A few miles upstream are Niagara Falls. Visitors can stand at their brink as the water tumbles 170 feet (52 meters) over the escarpment, and the *Maid of the Mist* sails right up to their base. There are viewing tunnels underneath the falls, and observation towers above them. A newly built attraction is a butterfly house.

Just a few of the Thousand Islands

GLOSSARY

becalmed (buh KAHLMD) — not moving because of lack of wind

confederacy (kun FED uh ruh see) — a group joined for a common purpose

habitat (HAB uh tat) — the kind of place where an animal or plant lives

interpreter (in TUR pruh tur) — A person who explains a way of life through acting

lamprey (LAM pree) — an eel-like creature preying on fish

loyalist (LOY uhl ist) — one loyal to the British Crown during the American Revolution

Niagara escarpment (ni AG ruh eh SKARP munt) — a line of steep cliffs stretching north from Niagara Falls

process (PRAH ses) — to make a raw material into a usable form

skirmish (SKUR mish) — a short fight between small forces

strategic (struh TEE jik) — important because of its position

Kayaking on a summer's day

INDEX

canals   5, 14, 29

forts   14, 26, 29

Hamilton   14, 17

native peoples   9

New York State   5, 6, 26, 29

Niagara   5, 14, 22, 29

Ontario   5, 8, 13, 25

Oswego   5, 20, 24, 29

rivers   5, 8, 16

Rochester   16, 18, 20

Thousand Islands   21, 25, 26

Toronto   6, 13, 18, 21, 22

water transportation   18

FURTHER READING

You can find out more about the Great Lakes with these helpful books and web sites:
- Ruth Graber. *The Unknown Story of 1000 World War II Refugees*
- Pierre Berton. *The Great Lakes*
- Bill Lund. *The Iroquois Indians,* Bridgestone Books
- Virginia Driving Hawk Sneve. *The Iroquois,* Holiday House
- The Penfield Library, State University of New York at Oswego

- www.visit1000islands.com
- www.techdiver.com/html
- www.boldtcastle.com/history.htm
- www.rom.on.ca
- The Chambers of Commerce, Sackets Harbor: www.co.oswego.ny.us
- Rochester and Oswego Seagrant: www.seagr.wisc.edu/greatlakes
- The Nature Conservancy: www.tnc.org/infield/State/programs/regional/elo.htm
- Great Lakes Information Network: www.great-lakes.net
- Quizzes on the Lakes : www.hcbe.edu.on.ca/coll/lakes.htm